Inspiration
PRIDE PARADE
Poetry & Quotes

Publisher and Creative Director: Nick Wells
Editorial Assistant: Taylor Bentley
Art Director: Mike Spender
Layout Design: Jane Ashley
Digital Design and Production: Chris Herbert

FLAME TREE PUBLISHING
6 Melbray Mews
London SW6 3NS
United Kingdom

www.flametreepublishing.com
First published 2020

20 21 22 23 24
1 3 5 7 9 10 8 6 4 2

© 2020 Flame Tree Publishing

All rights reserved. No part of this publication may be reproduced, stored in a retrieval system, or transmitted in any form or by any means, electronic, mechanical, photocopying, recording or otherwise, without prior permission in writing of the publisher.

Every effort has been made to contact copyright holders. In the event of an oversight the publishers would be glad to rectify any omissions in future editions of this book.

A CIP record for this book is available from the British Library upon request.

ISBN 978-1-83964-161-9

Printed in China | Created, Developed & Produced in the United Kingdom

Inspiration
PRIDE PARADE
Poetry & Quotes

Introduction by
Sarah Parker

FLAME TREE
PUBLISHING

Contents

Introduction
6

Beauty & Desire
10

Love & Intimacy
44

Loss & Isolation
82

Identity & Acceptance
118

Index
158

Introduction

In his poem 'Two Loves' of 1892, Lord Alfred Douglas – the lover of Oscar Wilde – famously described homosexual love as 'the love that dare not speak its name'. However, the poems in this collection prove that in fact, quite the opposite was true. If we search through literary history, we will find endless examples of such love daring to 'speak its name'. Indeed, poetry was the ideal form for articulating such love. With its mysterious symbolism, evocative imagery and fluid identities – the poetic 'I' speaker and the 'you' addressee could be just about anyone – poetry provided a way of expressing LGBT experience for those 'in the know' without risking spelling out one's meaning too explicitly.

From passionate poems of desire and lust, to heartful celebrations of life-long partnership, this anthology reveals that poets have been expressing queer love in all its forms for many centuries. The poems and prose extracts in this anthology span from antiquity to the early twentieth century, and yet they deal with aspects of experience and identity that will resonate with readers today.
The first section on Beauty and Desire includes Sappho's famous 'Ode to Anactoria', describing the speaker's overwhelming desire for a woman who sits nearby, speaking to a man. Composed

around the seventh century BC, this poem expresses strikingly physical longing and jealousy. Sappho's work survives in fragments and, for centuries, translators changed the pronouns of female addressees to male, in order to present Sappho as straightforwardly heterosexual. Nonetheless, her work proved inspiring to later poets. We can detect her influence in Alice Dunbar Nelson's brief, flame-like poem 'You! Inez!' which ardently addresses a woman lover who stirs 'the depths of passionate desire'. Meanwhile, Oscar Wilde's *The Picture of Dorian Gray* reveals to us that the late-Victorian 'Cult of Beauty' provided a language to articulate male homoerotic love.

The following section on Love and Intimacy explores lasting partnerships, beyond the first stirrings of desire. In their poem 'It was deep April and the morn', Katharine Bradley and Edith Cooper, collaborating under the pseudonym 'Michael Field' celebrate their lifelong companionship as 'poets and lovers', in defiance of the world's judgment. Meanwhile, Radclyffe Hall whimsically ponders finding a love-nest in her playful poem 'House Hunting' – a contrast to her notoriously dour novel *The Well of Loneliness*. Amy Lowell's poem 'A Decade' marks this anniversary by comparing the early taste of desire, 'red wine and honey' to the later savour of 'morning bread' which is ultimately more nourishing. Many of these poems convey a need to protect and honour misunderstood love in a difficult, dangerous world – perhaps none more so than Countee Cullen's 'Tableau' which describes the 'black boy and the white' locked arm-in-arm, defying those who are:

> *Indignant that these two should dare*
> *In unison to walk.*

The third section on Loss and Isolation describes the devastation of losing a loved one and the pain of separation. A. E. Housman's heart-breaking 'He would not stay for me, and who can wonder' conveys the agony of unrequited love which leaves the speaker feeling half-alive. Amy Levy's mysterious poem 'On the Threshold' envisions a bereavement in which the speaker is unable to kiss or embrace the dead beloved – death does not overcome the boundary that stands between them. Finally, Wilfred Owen's poems remind us of the mass losses of the Great War, while Wilde's 'The Ballad of Reading Gaol' evokes the persecution suffered by those condemned for so-called acts of 'gross indecency'.

The final section, Identity and Acceptance, reaffirms the courage of these writers as they bravely asserted their identity in the face of hostile society. Claude McKay's 'I Know My Soul' explores the importance of self-knowledge without judgement:

> *If I can comprehend but not control,*
> *I need not gloom my days with futile dread*

Jennie June's pioneering *Autobiography of an Androgyne* boldly claims the acceptance of God for the transgender individual. Finally, Walt Whitman's impassioned 'Song of Myself' ecstatically declares: 'Divine am I inside and out, and I make holy whatever I touch or am touch'd from'. Whitman's words of radical self-love and self-acceptance are surely the very definition of pride, and their power reverberates in our own cultural moment.

Sarah Parker

Sarah Parker is a lecturer in English at Loughborough University. She is the author of *The Lesbian Muse and Poetic Identity, 1889–1930* and co-editor of *Michael Field: Decadent Moderns*. She has published articles on writers including Olive Custance, Amy Levy and Djuna Barnes.

Beauty & Desire

Anactoria (extract)

My life is bitter with thy love; thine eyes
Blind me, thy tresses burn me, thy sharp sighs
Divide my flesh and spirit with soft sound,
And my blood strengthens, and my veins abound.
I pray thee sigh not, speak not, draw not breath;
Let life burn down, and dream it is not death.
I would the sea had hidden us, the fire
(Wilt thou fear that, and fear not my desire?)
Severed the bones that bleach, the flesh that cleaves,
And let our sifted ashes drop like leaves.
I feel thy blood against my blood: my pain
Pains thee, and lips bruise lips, and vein stings vein.
Let fruit be crushed on fruit, let flower on flower,
Breast kindle breast, and either burn one hour.
Why wilt thou follow lesser loves? are thine
Too weak to bear these hands and lips of mine?
I charge thee for my life's sake, O too sweet
To crush love with thy cruel faultless feet,

I charge thee keep thy lips from hers or his,
Sweetest, till theirs be sweeter than my kiss:
Lest I too lure, a swallow for a dove,
Erotion or Erinna to my love.

Algernon Charles Swinburne (1837–1909)

You! Inez!

Orange gleams athwart a crimson soul
Lambent flames; purple passion lurks
In your dusk eyes.
Red mouth; flower soft,
Your soul leaps up–and flashes
Star-like, white, flame-hot.
Curving arms, encircling a world of love,
You! Stirring the depths of passionate desire!

Alice Dunbar-Nelson (1875–1935)

I Sit and Sew

I sit and sew–a useless task it seems,
My hands grown tired, my head weighed down with dreams–
The panoply of war, the martial tred of men,
Grim-faced, stern-eyed, gazing beyond the ken
Of lesser souls, whose eyes have not seen Death,
Nor learned to hold their lives but as a breath–
But–I must sit and sew.

I sit and sew–my heart aches with desire–
That pageant terrible, that fiercely pouring fire
On wasted fields, and writhing grotesque things
Once men. My soul in pity flings
Appealing cries, yearning only to go
There in that holocaust of hell, those fields of woe–
But–I must sit and sew.

The little useless seam, the idle patch;
Why dream I here beneath my homely thatch,
When there they lie in sodden mud and rain,
Pitifully calling me, the quick ones and the slain?

You need me, Christ! It is no roseate dream
That beckons me–this pretty futile seam,
It stifles me–God, must I sit and sew?

Alice Dunbar-Nelson (1875–1935)

At a Dinner Party

With fruit and flowers the board is decked,
The wine and laughter flow;
I'll not complain–could one expect
  So dull a world to know?

You look across the fruit and flowers,
  My glance your glances find.–
It is our secret, only ours,
  Since all the world is blind.

Amy Levy (1861–89)

Alfonso, Dressing to Wait at a Table

Alfonso is a handsome bronze-hued lad
Of subtly-changing and surprising parts;
His moods are storms that frighten and make glad,
His eyes were made to capture women's hearts.

Down in the glory-hole Alfonso sings
An olden song of wine and clinking glasses
And riotous rakes; magnificently flings
Gay kisses to imaginary lasses.

Alfonso's voice of mellow music thrills
Our swaying forms and steals our hearts with joy;
And when he soars, his fine falsetto trills
Are rarest notes of gold without alloy.

But, O Alfonso! wherefore do you sing
Dream-songs of carefree men and ancient places?
Soon we shall be beset by clamouring
Of hungry and importunate palefaces.

Claude McKay (1889–1948)

Epitaphs

For a Fool
On earth the wise man makes the rules,
And is the fool's adviser,
But here the wise are as the fools,
(And no man is the wiser).

For One Who Gaily Sowed His Oats
My days were a thing for me to live,
For others to deplore;
I took of life all it could give;
Rind, inner fruit, and core.

For a Wanton
To men no more than so much cover
For them to doff or try,
I found in death a constant lover;
Here in his arms I lie.

For a Preacher
Vanity of vanitites,
All is vanity; yea,
Even the rod He flayed you with
Crumbled and turned to clay

Countee Cullen (1903–46)

WILD NIGHTS – WILD NIGHTS!

Wild Nights – Wild Nights!
Were I with thee
Wild Nights should be
Our luxury!

Futile – the winds –
To a heart in port –
Done with the compass –
Done with the chart!

Rowing in Eden –
Ah, the sea!
Might I moor – Tonight –
In thee!

Emily Dickinson (1830–86)

Lifting Belly (extract)

Kiss my lips. She did.

Kiss my lips again she did.

Kiss my lips over and over and over again she did.

I have feathers.

Gentle fishes.

Do you think about apricots. We find them very beautiful.

It is not alone their color it is their seeds that charm us. We find it a change.

Lifting belly is so strange.

I came to speak about it.

Selected raisins well their grapes grapes are good.

Change your name.

Question and garden.

It's raining. Don't speak about it.

My baby is a dumpling. I want to tell her something. Wax candles. We have bought a great many wax candles. Some are decorated. They have not been lighted.

I do not mention roses.

Exactly.

Actually.

Question and butter.

I find the butter very good.

Lifting belly is so kind.
Lifting belly fattily.
Doesn't that astonish you.
You did want me.
Say it again.
Strawberry.
Lifting beside belly.
Lifting lindly belly.
Sing to me I say.
Some are wives not heroes.
Lifting belly merely.
Sing to me I say.
Lifting belly. A reflection.
Lifting belly adjoibs more prizes.
Fit to be.
I have fit on a hat.
Have you.
What did you say to excuse me. Difficult paper and scattered.
Lifting belly is so kind.

Gertrude Stein (1874–1946)

Pink Melon Joy (extract)

Fourteen days.
I meant to be closeted.
I should have been thin.
I was aching.
I saw all the rose. I do mostly think that there is politeness. All of it on leather. Not it. I shall speak of it. I so mean to be dried. In the retracting glory there is more choice. There is what was threaded. I don't mean permitting.
Webster.
Little reinforced Susan.
Actual.
Actual believe me.
I see it all.
Why shouldn't I.
Lizzie Make Us.
I believe it.
Why shall I polite it. Pilot it.
Eleven o'clock.
Pillow.
I meant to say.

Saturday.

Not polite.

Do satisfy me.

This is to say that baby is all well. That baby is baby. That baby is all well. That there is a piano. That baby is all well. This is to say that baby is all well. This is to say that baby is all well.

Selling.

She has always said she was comfortable.

Was the water hot.

Gertrude Stein (1874–1946)

SUSIE ASADO

Sweet sweet sweet sweet sweet tea.

Susie Asado.

Sweet sweet sweet sweet sweet tea.

Susie Asado.

Susie Asado which is a told tray sure.

A lean on the shoe this means slips slips hers.

When the ancient light grey is clean it is yellow, it is a
    silver seller.

This is a please this is a please there are the saids to jelly.

These are the wets these say the sets to leave a crown to Incy.

Incy is short for incubus.

A pot. A pot is a beginning of a rare bit of trees. Trees
    tremble, the old vats are in bobbles, bobbles which shade
    and shove and render clean, render clean must.

Drink pups.

Drink pups drink pups lease a sash hold, see it shine and a
bobolink has pins. It shows a nail.

What is a nail. A nail is unison.

Sweet sweet sweet sweet sweet tea.

Gertrude Stein (1874–1946)

The Iliad (extract)

Godlike Ganymedes that was born the fairest of mortal men; wherefore the gods caught him up on high to be cupbearer to Zeus by reason of his beauty, that he might dwell with the immortals.

Homer (*c.* 700–600 BC)
Translation by A.T. Murray (1866–1940)

The Picture of Dorian Gray (extract)

'And yet,' continued Lord Henry, in his low, musical voice, and with that graceful wave of the hand that was always so characteristic of him, and that he had even in his Eton days, 'I believe that if one man were to live out his life fully and completely, were to give form to every feeling, expression to every thought, reality to every dream – I believe that the world would gain such a fresh impulse of joy that we would forget all the maladies of mediaevalism, and return to the Hellenic ideal – to something finer, richer than the Hellenic ideal, it may be. But the bravest man amongst us is afraid of himself. The mutilation of the savage has its tragic survival in the self-denial that mars our lives. We are punished for our refusals. Every impulse that we strive to strangle broods in the mind and poisons us. The body sins once, and has done with its sin, for action is a mode of purification. Nothing remains then but the recollection of a pleasure, or the luxury of a regret. The only way to get rid of a temptation is to yield to it. Resist it, and your soul grows sick with longing for the things it has forbidden to itself, with desire for what its monstrous laws have made monstrous and unlawful. It has been said that the great events of the world take place in the brain. It is in the brain, and the brain only, that the great sins of the world take place also. You, Mr. Gray, you yourself, with your rose-red youth and your rose-white boyhood, you have had passions that have made you afraid, thoughts that have filled you with terror, day-dreams and sleeping dreams whose mere memory might stain your cheek with shame—'

'Stop!' faltered Dorian Gray, 'stop! you bewilder me. I don't know what to say. There is some answer to you, but I cannot find it. Don't speak. Let me think. Or, rather, let me try not to think.'

Oscar Wilde (1854–1900)

ONE NIGHT

I stood beside you in the dark,
And felt the magic of the night
Steal o'er my senses, 'til they swooned,
And mists of passion dimmed my sight.
The stillness made me dumb, those words
I dared not utter choked my breath,
Each crushing each, as mad with life
They rose, to die a silent death.
My lips grew dry beneath the fire
Of kisses that they feign would give,
And every pulse, with answering beat,
Throbbed in its eagerness to live.

Radclyffe Hall (1880–1943)

TO SOME ONE!

Why kinder to the breeze than unto me?
For oft you let him play within your hair,
Blow its soft curls about, and find it fair,
The while he whispers low and tenderly
Into your ear; and yet how cold is he!
And loves you not, but only frolics there;
Sometimes I wish I might be turned to air,
And thus be rid of my humanity,
That finds no favour in your haughty eyes.
Were I a breeze you'd fling your windows wide,
And give me welcome, as I swept aside
The curtain, kissing all pride now denies,
Your lips, your cheeks, your eyes, your throat, your breast,
Until with kissing spent I sank to rest.

Radclyffe Hall (1880–1943)

Sonnet 17

Cherry-lipt Adonis in his snowie shape,
Might not compare with his pure ivorie white,
On whose faire front a poet's pen may write,
Whose roseate red excels the crimson grape,
His love-enticing delicate soft limbs,
Are rarely fram'd t'intrap poore gazine eies:
His cheeks, the lillie and carnation dies,
With lovely tincture which Apollo's dims.
His lips ripe strawberries in nectar wet,
His mouth a Hive, his tongue a hony-combe,
Where Muses (like bees) make their mansion.
His teeth pure pearle in blushing correll set.
Oh how can such a body sinne-procuring,
Be slow to love, and quicke to hate, enduring?

Richard Barnfield (1574–1627)

Ode to Anactoria

Peer of Gods to me is the man thy presence
Crowns with joy; who hears, as he sits beside thee,
Accents sweet of thy lips the silence breaking,
With lovely laughter;

Tones that make the heart in my bosom flutter,
For if I, the space of a moment even,
Near to thee come, any word I would utter
Instantly fails me;

Vain my stricken tongue would a whisper fashion,
Subtly under my skin runs fire ecstatic;
Straightway mists surge dim to my eyes and leave them
Reft of their vision;

Echoes ring in my ears; a trembling seizes
All my body bathed in soft perspiration;
Pale as grass I grow in my passion's madness,
Like one insensate;

But must I dare all, since to me unworthy,
Bliss thy beauty brings that a God might envy;
Never yet was fervid woman a fairer
Image of Kypris.

Ah! undying Daughter of God, befriend me!
Calm my blood that thrills with impending transport;
Feed my lips the murmur of words to stir her
Bosom to pity;

Overcome with kisses her faintest protest,
Melt her mood to mine with amorous touches,
Till her low assent and her sigh's abandon
Lure me to rapture.

Sappho (b. 620 BC)
Translation by John Myers O'Hara (1870–1944)

The Daughter of Cyprus

Dreaming I spake with the Daughter of Cyprus,
Heard the languor soft of her voice, the blended
Suave accord of tones interfused with laughter
Low and desireful;

Dreaming saw her dread ineffable beauty,
Saw through texture fine of her clinging tunic
Blush the fire of flesh, the rose of her body,
Radiant, blinding;

Saw through filmy meshes the melting lovely
Flow of line, the exquisite curves, whence piercing
Rapture reached with tangible touch to thrill me,
Almost to slay me;

Saw the gleaming foot, and the golden sandal
Held by straps of Lydian work thrice doubled
Over the instep's arch, and up the rounded
Dazzling ankle;

Saw the charms that shimmered from knee to shoulder,
Hint of hues, than milk or the snowdrift whiter;
Secret grace, the shrine of the soul of passion,
Glows that consumed me;

Saw the gathered mass of her xanthic tresses,
Mitra-bound, escape from the clasping fillet,
Float and shine as clouds in the sunset splendor,
Mists in the dawn-fire;

Saw the face immortal, and daring greatly,
Raised my eyes to hers of unfathomed azure,
Drank their world's desire, their limitless longing,
Swooned and was nothing.

Sappho (b. 620 BC)
Translation by John Myers O'Hara (1870–1944)

Song of Myself: 11 (extract)

Twenty-eight young men bathe by the shore,
Twenty-eight young men and all so friendly;
Twenty-eight years of womanly life and all so lonesome.

She owns the fine house by the rise of the bank,
She hides handsome and richly drest aft the blinds of the window.

Which of the young men does she like the best?
Ah the homeliest of them is beautiful to her.

Where are you off to, lady? for I see you,
You splash in the water there, yet stay stock still in your room.

Dancing and laughing along the beach came the twenty-ninth bather,
The rest did not see her, but she saw them and loved them.

The beards of the young men glisten'd with wet, it ran from their long hair,
Little streams pass'd all over their bodies.

An unseen hand also pass'd over their bodies,
It descended tremblingly from their temples and ribs.

The young men float on their backs, their white bellies bulge to the
sun, they do not ask who seizes fast to them,
They do not know who puffs and declines with pendant and bending arch,
They do not think whom they souse with spray.

Walt Whitman (1819–92)

I Sing the Body Electric! (extract)

1
I sing the body electric,
The armies of those I love engirth me and I engirth them,
They will not let me off till I go with them, respond to them,
And discorrupt them, and charge them full with the charge of the soul.

Was it doubted that those who corrupt their own bodies conceal themselves?
And if those who defile the living are as bad as they who defile the dead?
And if the body does not do fully as much as the soul?
And if the body were not the soul, what is the soul?

2
The love of the body of man or woman balks account, the body itself balks account,
That of the male is perfect, and that of the female is perfect.

The expression of the face balks account,
But the expression of a well-made man appears not only in his face,

It is in his limbs and joints also, it is curiously in the joints
 of his hips and wrists,
It is in his walk, the carriage of his neck, the flex of his
 waist and knees, dress does not hide him,
The strong sweet quality he has strikes through the cotton
 and broadcloth,
To see him pass conveys as much as the best poem,
 perhaps more,
You linger to see his back, and the back of his neck and
 shoulder-side.

The sprawl and fulness of babes, the bosoms and heads of
 women, the folds of their dress, their style as we pass in
 the street, the contour of their shape downwards,
The swimmer naked in the swimming-bath, seen as he swims
 through the transparent green-shine, or lies with his
 face up and rolls silently to and fro in the heave of the water,
The bending forward and backward of rowers in row-boats,
 the horseman in his saddle,
Girls, mothers, house-keepers, in all their performances,
The group of laborers seated at noon-time with their open
 dinner-kettles, and their wives waiting,
The female soothing a child, the farmer's daughter in the
garden or cow-yard,

The young fellow hoeing corn, the sleigh-driver driving his
    six horses through the crowd,
The wrestle of wrestlers, two apprentice-boys, quite grown,
    lusty, good-natured, native-born, out on the vacant lot
    at sun-down after work,
The coats and caps thrown down, the embrace of love
    and resistance,
The upper-hold and under-hold, the hair rumpled over and
    blinding the eyes;
The march of firemen in their own costumes, the play of
masculine muscle through clean-setting trowsers and
    waist-straps,
The slow return from the fire, the pause when the bell
    strikes suddenly again, and the listening on the alert,
The natural, perfect, varied attitudes, the bent head, the
    curv'd neck and the counting;
Such-like I love–I loosen myself, pass freely, am at the
    mother's breast with the little child,
Swim with the swimmers, wrestle with wrestlers, march in
    line with the firemen, and pause, listen, count.

Walt Whitman (1819–92)

Sonnet

Alas, that June should come when thou didst go;
I think you passed each other on the way;
And seeing thee, the Summer loved thee so
That all her loveliness she gave away;
Her rare perfumes, in hawthorn boughs distilled,
Blushing, she in thy sweeter bosom left,
Thine arms with all her virgin roses filled,
Yet felt herself the richer for thy theft;
Beggared herself of morning for thine eyes,
Hung on the lips of every bird the tune,
Breathed on thy cheek her soft vermilion dyes,
And in thee set the singing heart of June.
And so, not only do I mourn thy flight,
But Summer comes despoiled of her delight.

Willa Cather (1873–1947)

Sonnet 20

A woman's face with Nature's own hand painted
Hast thou, the master-mistress of my passion;
A woman's gentle heart, but not acquainted
With shifting change, as is false women's fashion;
An eye more bright than theirs, less false in rolling,
Gilding the object whereupon it gazeth;
A man in hue, all 'hues' in his controlling,
Which steals men's eyes and women's souls amazeth.
And for a woman wert thou first created;
Till Nature, as she wrought thee, fell a-doting,
And by addition me of thee defeated,
By adding one thing to my purpose nothing.
But since she prick'd thee out for women's pleasure,
Mine be thy love and thy love's use their treasure.

William Shakespeare (1564–1616)

Sonnet 144

Two loves I have of comfort and despair,
Which like two spirits do suggest me still
The better angel is a man right fair,
The worser spirit a woman coloured ill.
To win me soon to hell, my female evil
Tempteth my better angel from my side,
And would corrupt my saint to be a devil,
Wooing his purity with her foul pride.
And, whether that my angel be turn'd fiend,
Suspect I may, yet not directly tell,
But being both from me both to each friend,
I guess one angel in another's hell.
Yet this shall I ne'er know, but live in doubt,
Till my bad angel fire my good one out.

William Shakespeare (1564–1616)

Love & Intimacy

A Shropshire Lad – XVIII

Oh, when I was in love with you,
Then I was clean and brave,
And miles around the wonder grew
How well did I behave.

And now the fancy passes by,
And nothing will remain,
And miles around they'll say that I
Am quite myself again.

A.E. Housman (1859–1936)

Hora Stellatrix

The stars hang thick in the apple tree,
The south wind smells of the pungent sea,
Gold tulip cups are heavy with dew.
The night's for you, Sweetheart, for you!
Starfire rains from the vaulted blue.

Listen! The dancing of unseen leaves.
A drowsy swallow stirs in the eaves.
Only a maiden is sorrowing.
'Tis night and spring, Sweetheart, and spring!
Starfire lights your heart's blossoming.

In the intimate dark there's never an ear,
Though the tulips stand on tiptoe to hear,
So give; ripe fruit must shrivel or fall.
As you are mine, Sweetheart, give all!
Starfire sparkles, your coronal.

Amy Lowell (1874-1925)

A Decade

When you came, you were like red wine and honey,
And the taste of you burnt my mouth with its sweetness.
Now you are like morning bread,
Smooth and pleasant.
I hardly taste you at all for I know your savour,
But I am completely nourished.

Amy Lowell (1874–1925)

Llangollen Vale (extract)

Now with a vestal lustre glows the vale,
Thine, sacred FRIENDSHIP, permanent as pure;
In vain the stern Authorities assail,
In vain Persuasion spreads her silken lure,
High-born, and high-endow'd, the peerless Twain,
Pant for coy Nature's charms 'mid silent dale, and plain.

Thro' ELEANORA, and her ZARA'S mind,
Early tho'genius, taste, and fancy flow'd,
Tho' all the graceful Arts their powers combin'd,
And her last polish brilliant Life bestow'd,
The lavish Promiser, in Youth's soft morn,
Pride, Pomp, and Love, her friends, the sweet Enthusiasts scorn.

Then rose the Fairy Palace of the Vale,
Then bloom'd around it the Arcadian bowers;
Screen'd from the storms of Winter, cold and pale,
Screen'd from the fervours of the sultry hours,
Circling the lawny crescent, soon they rose,
To letter'd ease devote, and Friendship's blest repose.

Smiling they rose beneath the plastic hand
Of Energy, and Taste; – nor only they,
Obedient Science hears the mild command,
Brings every gift that speeds the tardy day,
Whate'er the pencil sheds in vivid hues,
Th' historic tome reveals, or sings the raptured Muse.

How sweet to enter, at the twilight grey,
The dear, minute Lyceum of the Dome,
When, thro' the colour'd crystal, glares the ray,
Sanguine and solemn 'mid the gathering gloom,
While glow-worm lamps diffuse a pale, green light,
Such as in mossy lanes illume the starless night.

Then the coy Scene, by deep'ning veils o'erdrawn,
In shadowy elegance seems lovelier still;
Tall shrubs, that skirt the semi-lunar lawn,
Dark woods, that curtain the opposing hill;
While o'er their brows the bare cliff faintly gleams,
And, from its paly edge, the evening-diamond streams.

Anna Seward (1742–1809)

Joseph and His Friend: A Story of Pennsylvania (extract)

They took each other's hands. The day was fading, the landscape was silent, and only the twitter of nesting birds was heard in the boughs above them. Each gave way to the impulse of his manly love, rarer, alas! but as tender and true as the love of woman, and they drew nearer and kissed each other. As they walked back and parted on the highway, each felt that life was not wholly unkind, and that happiness was not yet impossible.

Bayard Taylor (1825–78)

Love Returned

He was a boy when first we met;
His eyes were mixed of dew and fire,
And on his candid brow was set
The sweetness of a chaste desire:
But in his veins the pulses beat
Of passion, waiting for its wing,
As ardent veins of summer heat
Throb through the innocence of spring.

As manhood came, his stature grew,
And fiercer burned his restless eyes,
Until I trembled, as he drew
From wedded hearts their young disguise.
Like wind-fed flame his ardor rose,
And brought, like flame, a stormy rain:
In tumult, sweeter than repose,
He tossed the souls of joy and pain.

So many years of absence change!
I knew him not when he returned:
His step was slow, his brow was strange,

His quiet eye no longer burned.
When at my heart I heard his knock,
No voice within his right confessed:
I could not venture to unlock
Its chambers to an alien guest.

Then, at the threshold, spent and worn
With fruitless travel, down he lay:
And I beheld the gleams of morn
On his reviving beauty play.
I knelt, and kissed his holy lips,
I washed his feet with pious care;
And from my life the long eclipse
Drew off; and left his sunshine there.

He burns no more with youthful fire;
He melts no more in foolish tears;
Serene and sweet, his eyes inspire
The steady faith of balanced years.
His folded wings no longer thrill,
But in some peaceful flight of prayer:
He nestles in my heart so still,
I scarcely feel his presence there.

O Love, that stern probation o'er,
Thy calmer blessing is secure!
Thy beauteous feet shall stray no more,
Thy peace and patience shall endure!
The lightest wind deflowers the rose,
The rainbow with the sun departs,
But thou art centred in repose,
And rooted in my heart of hearts!

Bayard Taylor (1825–78)

On the Road to the Sea

We passed each other, turned and stopped for half an
hour, then went our way,
I who make other women smile did not make you –
But no man can move mountains in a day.
So this hard thing is yet to do.

But first I want your life: – before I die I want to see
The world that lies behind the strangeness of your eyes,
There is nothing gay or green there for my gathering,
it may be,
Yet on brown fields there lies
A haunting purple bloom: is there not something in
grey skies
And in grey sea?
I want what world there is behind your eyes,
I want your life and you will not give it me.

Now, if I look, I see you walking down the years,
Young, and through August fields – a face, a thought, a
swinging dream
perched on a stile – ;
I would have liked (so vile we are!) to have taught you tears

But most to have made you smile.
To-day is not enough or yesterday: God sees it all –
Your length on sunny lawns, the wakeful rainy nights – ;
tell me – ;
(how vain to ask), but it is not a question – just a call – ;
Show me then, only your notched inches climbing up the garden wall,
I like you best when you are small.

Is this a stupid thing to say
Not having spent with you one day?
No matter; I shall never touch your hair
Or hear the little tick behind your breast,
Still it is there,
And as a flying bird
Brushes the branches where it may not rest
I have brushed your hand and heard
The child in you: I like that best
So small, so dark, so sweet; and were you also then too grave and wise?
Always I think. Then put your far off little hand in mine; –
Oh! let it rest;

I will not stare into the early world beyond the opening eyes,
Or vex or scare what I love best.
But I want your life before mine bleeds away –
Here – not in heavenly hereafters – soon, –
I want your smile this very afternoon,
(The last of all my vices, pleasant people used to say,
I wanted and I sometimes got – the Moon!)

You know, at dusk, the last bird's cry,
And round the house the flap of the bat's low flight,
Trees that go black against the sky
And then – how soon the night!

No shadow of you on any bright road again,
And at the darkening end of this – what voice? whose kiss? As if you'd say!
It is not I who have walked with you, it will not be I who take away
Peace, peace, my little handful of the gleaner's grain
From your reaped fields at the shut of day.

Peace! Would you not rather die
Reeling, – with all the cannons at your ear?

So, at least, would I,
And I may not be here
To-night, to-morrow morning or next year.
Still I will let you keep your life a little while,
See dear?
I have made you smile.

Charlotte Mew (1869–1928)

ABSENCE

Your words dropped into my heart like pebbles into a pool,
Rippling around my breast and leaving it melting cool.

Your kisses fell sharp on my flesh like dawn-dews from the limb,
Of a fruit-filled lemon tree when the day is young and dim.

But a silence vasty-deep, oh deeper than all these ties
Now, through the menacing miles, brooding between us lies.

And more than the songs I sing, I await your written word,
To stir my fluent blood as never your presence stirred.

Claude McKay (1889–1948)

TORMENTED

I will not reason, wrestle here with you,
Though you pursue and worry me about;
As well put forth my swarthy arm to stop
The wild wind howling, darkly mad without.

The night is yours for revels; day will light.
I will not fight you, bold and tigerish,
For I am weak, while you are gaining strength;
Peace! cease tormenting me to have your wish.

But when you're filled and sated with the flesh,
I shall go swiftly to the silver stream,
To cleanse my body for the spirit's sake,
And sun my limbs, and close my eyes to dream.

Claude McKay (1889–1948)

Courage

O lonely heart so timid of approach,
Like the shy tropic flower that shuts its lips
To the faint touch of tender finger tips:
What is your word? What question would you broach?

Your lustrous-warm eyes are too sadly kind
To mask the meaning of your dreamy tale,
Your guarded life too exquisitely frail
Against the daggers of my warring mind.

There is no part of the unyielding earth,
Even bare rocks where the eagles build their nest,
Will give us undisturbed and friendly rest.
No dewfall softens this vast belt of dearth.

But in the socket-chiseled teeth of strife,
That gleam in serried files in all the lands,
We may join hungry, understanding hands,
And drink our share of ardent love and life.

Claude McKay (1889–1948)

TABLEAU (FOR DONALD DUFF)

Locked arm in arm they cross the way
The black boy and the white,
The golden splendor of the day
The sable pride of night.

From lowered blinds the dark folk stare
And here the fair folk talk,
Indignant that these two should dare
In unison to walk.

Oblivious to look and word
They pass, and see no wonder
That lightning brilliant as a sword
Should blaze the path of thunder.

Countee Cullen (1903–46)

E.M. Forster on Maurice

A happy ending was imperative. I shouldn't have bothered to write otherwise. I was determined that in fiction anyway two men should fall in love and remain in it for the ever and ever that fiction allows, and in this sense, Maurice and Alec still roam the greenwood.

E.M. Forster (1879–1970)

Letter to Susan Huntington Gilbert Dickinson (extract)

I have but one thought, Susie, this afternoon of June, and that of you, and I have one prayer, only; dear Susie, that is for you. That you and I in hand as we e'en do in heart, might ramble away as children, among the woods and fields, and forget these many years, and these sorrowing cares, and each become a child again – I would it were so, Susie, and when I look around me and find myself alone, I sigh for you again; little sigh, and vain sigh, which will not bring you home.

I need you more and more, and the great world grows wider, and dear ones fewer and fewer, every day that you stay away – I miss my biggest heart; my own goes wandering round, and calls for Susie – Friends are too dear to sunder, Oh they are far too few, and how soon they will go away where you and I cannot find them, don't let us forget these things, for their remembrance now will save us many an anguish when it is too late to love them! Susie, forgive me Darling, for every word I say – my heart is full of you, none other than you is in my thoughts, yet when I seek to say to you something not for the world, words fail me. If you were here – and Oh that you were, my Susie, we need not talk at all, our eyes would whisper for us, and your hand fast in mine, we would not ask for language – I try to bring you nearer, I chase the weeks away till they are quite departed, and fancy you have come, and I am on my way through the green lane to meet you, and my heart goes scampering so, that I have much ado to bring it back again, and learn it to be patient, till that dear Susie comes. Three weeks – they can't last always, for surely they must go with their little brothers and sisters to their long home in the west!

I shall grow more and more impatient until that dear day comes, for till now, I have only mourned for you; now I begin to hope for you.

Emily Dickinson (1830–86)

Tell Her – the page I never wrote! (Version II)

Going – to – Her!
Happy – Letter! Tell Her–
Tell Her – the page I never wrote!
Tell Her, I only said – the Syntax –
And left the Verb and the Pronoun – out!
Tell Her just how the fingers – hurried –
Then – how they – stammered – slow – slow –
And then – you wished you had eyes – in your pages –
So you could see – what moved – them – so –

Tell Her – it wasn't a practised writer –
You guessed –
from the way the sentence – toiled –
You could hear the Bodice – tug – behind you –
As if it held but the might of a child!
You almost pitied – it – you – it worked so –
Tell Her–No – you may quibble – there –
For it would split Her Heart – to know it –
And then – you and I – were silenter!

Tell Her – Day – finished – before we – finished –
And the old Clock kept neighing – 'Day'!

And you – got sleepy – and begged to be ended–
What could – it hinder so – to say?
Tell Her – just how she sealed – you – Cautious!
But – if she ask 'where you are hid' – until the evening –
Ah! Be bashful!
Gesture Coquette –
And shake your Head!

Emily Dickinson (1830–86)

Her breast is fit for pearls

Her breast is fit for pearls,
But I was not a 'Diver' –
Her brow is fit for thrones
But I have not a crest.
Her heart is fit for home –
I – a Sparrow – build there
Sweet of twigs and twine
My perennial nest.

Emily Dickinson (1830–86)

To own a Susan of my own

To own a Susan of my own
Is of itself a Bliss –
Whatever Realm I forfeit, Lord,
Continue me in this!

Emily Dickinson (1830–86)

Letter to Jane Carlyle (extract)

Monday (Postmark, June 25, 1845)

Dearest Jane, – I want very much to know how you are, and how you are going on, though if you are in anything like my own state of body and soul letter-writing is precisely the most unpleasant thing in life. I think of you much. Those two weeks I spent with you are a great comfort to me. They seemed to give you back to me with all the freshness of the time when you wrote the first letter you ever wrote me. For the moment one says, 'I will be your friend,' and you accept it, it is an era quite as notable, and as much to be accounted of as if it were the lover to whom one gave oneself, body and soul, for ever! I was going to say perhaps it should be as long as he can retain one. However, I cannot tell you how thankful I feel to have you safe once more, because at one time I feared that perhaps the best period of our intercourse might be past; but you have shown both faith and patience towards me, and the time I was last with you seemed not the beginning of a new friendship, but rather what one might imagine to be the way we might meet in another life, after one had had the experience of a lifetime here to enlighten us on the follies and shortcomings of our friends. I care for you now more than ever I did, though I don't know why I am writing to tell you so; but I was lying on the sofa, where I have been all day, when an impulse stronger than my laziness made me get up. I could not help writing this to you. I know your birthday is either to-day or next Monday, but I have forgotten the exact day of the month, and I have been puzzling myself for the last three days; I think it will be next Monday, because —— says it will be, next Saturday, twelve months and a day since he sailed for Spain, and I know your birthday was the day but one following. So if I have mistaken, I have not forgotten.

Geraldine Jewsbury (1812–80)

An Account of The Ladies of Llangollen (extract)

July 15th, 1828

Before I left Llangollen I recollected the two celebrated ladies who have inhabited this valley for more than half a century, and of whom I had heard once as a child, and again recently in London. You have doubtless heard your father talk of them;–'si non, voilà leur histoire.' Fifty-six years ago, two young, pretty and fashionable ladies, Lady Eleanor Butler, and the daughter of the late Lord Ponsonby, took it in their heads to hate men, to love only each other, and to live from that hour in some remote hermitage. The resolution was immediately executed; and from that time neither lady has ever passed a night out of their cottage. On the other hand, no one who is presentable travels in Wales unprovided with an introduction to them. It is affirmed that the 'scandal' of the great world interests them as much as when they lived in it; and that their curiosity to know what passes has preserved all its freshness. I had compliments to deliver to them from several ladies, but I had neglected to furnish myself with a letter. I therefore sent my card, determined if they declined my visit, as I was led to fear, to storm the cottage. Here, as elsewhere, however, in England, a title easily opened the door, and I immediately received a gracious invitation to a second breakfast. Passing along a charming road, through a trim and pretty pleasure-ground, in a quarter of an hour I reached a small but tasteful gothic cottage, situated directly opposite to Dinas Bran, various glimpses of which were visible through openings cut in the trees. I alighted, and was received at the door by the two ladies. Fortunately I was already prepared by hearsay for their peculiarities; I might otherwise have found it difficult to repress some expression of astonishment. Imagine two ladies, the eldest of whom, Lady Eleanor, a short robust woman, begins to feel her years a little, being now eighty-three; the other, a tall and imposing person, esteems herself still youthful, being only seventy-four. Both wore their still abundant hair combed straight back and powdered, a round man's hat, a man's cravat and waistcoat, but in the place of 'inexpressibles,' a short petticoat and boots: the whole covered by a coat of blue cloth, of a cut quite peculiar,–a sort of middle term between a man's coat and a lady's riding-habit. Over this, Lady Eleanor wore, first, the grand cordon of the order of St. Louis across her shoulder; secondly, the same order around her neck; thirdly, the small cross of the same in her button-hole, and 'pour comble de gloire,' a golden lily of nearly the natural size, as a star,–all, as she said, presents of the Bourbon family. So far the whole effect was somewhat ludicrous. But now, you must imagine both ladies with that agreeable 'aisance,' that air of the world of the 'ancien regime,' courteous and entertaining, without the slightest affectation; speaking French as well as any Englishwoman of my acquaintance; and above all, with that essentially polite, unconstrained, and simply cheerful manner of the good society of that day, which, in our serious hardworking age of business, appears to be going to utter decay. I was really affected with a melancholy sort of pleasure in contemplating it in the persons of the amiable old ladies who are among the last of its living representatives; nor could I witness without lively sympathy the unremitting, natural and affectionate attention with which the younger treated her somewhat infirmer friend, and anticipated all her wants. The charm of such actions lies chiefly in the manner in which they are performed,–in things which appear small and insignificant, but which are never lost upon a susceptible heart.

Hermann, Fürst von Pückler-Muskau (1785–1871)

A Girl

A Girl,
Her soul a deep-wave pearl
Dim, lucent of all lovely mysteries;
A face flowered for heart's ease,
A brow's grace soft as seas
Seen through faint forest-trees:
A mouth, the lips apart,
Like aspen-leaflets trembling in the breeze
From her tempestuous heart.
Such: and our souls so knit,
I leave a page half-writ–
The work begun
Will be to heaven's conception done,
If she come to it.

Michael Field[1]

[1] Michael Field was the pseudonym used by collaborators and companions Katharine Bradley (1846–1914) and Edythe Cooper (1862–1913).

It Was Deep April

It was deep April, and the morn
Shakespeare was born;
The world was on us, pressing sore;
My love and I took hands and swore,
Against the world, to be
Poets and lovers evermore,
To laugh and dream on Lethe's shore,
To sing to Charon in his boat,
Heartening the timid souls afloat;
Of judgement never to take heed,
But to those fast-locked souls to speed,
Who never from Apollo fled,
Who spent no hour among the dead;
Continually
With them to dwell,
Indifferent to heaven and hell.

Michael Field

Unbosoming

The love that breeds
In my heart for thee!
As the iris is full, brimful of seeds,
And all that it flowered for among the reeds
Is packed in a thousand vermilion-beads
That push, and riot, and squeeze, and clip,
Till they burst the sides of the silver scrip,
And at last we see
What the bloom, with its tremulous, bowery fold
Of zephyr-petal at heart did hold:
So my breast is rent
With the burthen and strain of its great content;
For the summer of fragrance and sighs is dead,
The harvest-secret is burning red,
And I would give thee, after my kind,
The final issues of heart and mind.

Michael Field

On the Sale By Auction of Keats' Love Letters

These are the letters which Endymion wrote
To one he loved in secret, and apart.
And now the brawlers of the auction mart
Bargain and bid for each poor blotted note,
Ay! for each separate pulse of passion quote
The merchant's price. I think they love not art
Who break the crystal of a poet's heart
That small and sickly eyes may glare and gloat.

Is it not said that many years ago,
In a far Eastern town, some soldiers ran
With torches through the midnight, and began
To wrangel for mean raiment, and to throw
Dice for the garments of a wretched man,
Not knowing the God's wonder, or His woe?

Oscar Wilde (1854–1900)

House Hunting

Where shall we make us a cosy home,
Up in a high pine tree?
Suppose the squirrel deserts his nest,
And we could only grow small and rest
Under the twigs, laid so daintily,
Up in the high pine tree!

Where shall we build us a lovely house,
Under the Ocean deep?
Suppose the fishes would swim away,
And leave a palace of coral gay,
With seaweed gardens where moonbeams sleep,
Under the Ocean deep!

Where shall we find an enchanted spot,
Up in the fields of sky?
Suppose the rainbow bends slowly down,
And we walk over to Cloudy Town,
Golden with beams from the morning's eye,
Up in the fields of sky!

How shall we live out our days, we two,
Safely where no harm parts?
Suppose we fetter our lives with love,
More fair than ocean, or skies above,
And learn to dwell in each other's hearts,
Safely where no harm parts.

Radclyffe Hall (1880–1943)

The Meeting

To meet almost as strangers, who have been
Such lovers in the past! no glad delight
To thrill our senses, till the wrong seems right,
For very joy–I wonder will your mien
Be happy? it seems years since I have seen
You smiling! I shall take you to the light,
And trace new lines upon your brow, and right
Above them may be some gray hairs, your clean
Strong profile, will it look the very same?
Are your hands wrinkled? Oh! my perfect hands!
Be not less lovely now that passion stands
Aloof, and dare not kiss you into flame–
I could not bear it! Time can never blight
Such marvels, so divinely slim and white.

Radclyffe Hall (1880–1943)

THE WELL OF LONELINESS (EXTRACT)

Too late, too late, your love gave me life. Here am I the creature you made through your loving; by your passion you created the thing that I am. Who are you to deny me the right to love? But for you I need never have known existence.

Radclyffe Hall (1880–1943)

Loss & Isolation

He would not stay for me, and who can wonder

He would not stay for me, and who can wonder?
He would not stay for me to stand and gaze.
I shook his hand, and tore my heart in sunder,
And went with half my life about my ways.

A.E. Housman (1859–1936)

A Shropshire Lad – XV

Look not in my eyes, for fear
They mirror true the sight I see,
And there you find your face too clear
And love it and be lost like me.
One the long nights through must lie
Spent in star-defeated sighs,
But why should you as well as I
Perish? gaze not in my eyes.

A Grecian lad, as I hear tell,
One that many loved in vain,
Looked into a forest well
And never looked away again.
There, when the turf in springtime flowers,
With downward eye and gazes sad,
Stands amid the glancing showers
A jonquil, not a Grecian lad.

A.E. Housman (1859-1936)

A Shropshire Lad – XXXVIII

The winds out of the west land blow,
My friends have breathed them there;
Warm with the blood of lads I know
Comes east the sighing air.

It fanned their temples, filled their lungs,
Scattered their forelocks free;
My friends made words of it with tongues
That talk no more to me.

Their voices, dying as they fly,
Thick on the wind are sown;
The names of men blow soundless by,
My fellows' and my own.

Oh lads, at home I heard you plain,
But here your speech is still,
And down the sighing wind in vain
You hollo from the hill.

The wind and I, we both were there,
But neither long abode;
Now through the friendless world we fare
And sigh upon the road.

A.E. Housman (1859–1936)

A Shropshire Lad – XLIV

Shot? so quick, so clean an ending?
Oh that was right, lad, that was brave:
Yours was not an ill for mending,
'Twas best to take it to the grave.

Oh you had forethought, you could reason,
And saw your road and where it led,
And early wise and brave in season
Put the pistol to your head.

Oh soon, and better so than later
After long disgrace and scorn,
You shot dead the household traitor,
The soul that should not have been born.

Right you guessed the rising morrow
And scorned to tread the mire you must:
Dust's your wages, son of sorrow,
But men may come to worse than dust.

Souls undone, undoing others,-
Long time since the tale began.
You would not live to wrong your brothers:
Oh lad, you died as fits a man.

Now to your grave shall friend and stranger
With ruth and some with envy come:
Undishonoured, clear of danger,
Clean of guilt, pass hence and home.

Turn safe to rest, no dreams, no waking;
And here, man, here's the wreath I've made:
'Tis not a gift that's worth the taking,
But wear it and it will not fade.

A.E. Housman (1859–1936)

On the Threshold

O God, my dream! I dreamed that you were dead;
Your mother hung above the couch and wept
Whereon you lay all white, and garlanded
With blooms of waxen whiteness. I had crept
Up to your chamber-door, which stood ajar,
And in the doorway watched you from afar,
Nor dared advance to kiss your lips and brow.
I had no part nor lot in you, as now;
Death had not broken between us the old bar;
Nor torn from out my heart the old, cold sense
Of your misprision and my impotence.

Amy Levy (1861–89)

The Barrier

I must not gaze at them although
Your eyes are dawning day;
I must not watch you as you go
Your sun-illumined way;

I hear but I must never heed
The fascinating note,
Which, fluting like a river reed,
Comes from your trembing throat;

I must not see upon your face
Love's softly glowing spark;
For there's the barrier of race,
You're fair and I am dark.

Claude McKay (1889–1948)

A Song of Sour Grapes

I wish your body were in the grave,
Deep down as a grave may be,
Or rotting under the deepest wave
That ever ploughed the sea.

I wish I never had seen your face,
Or the sinuous curve of your mouth,
Dear as a straw to a man who drowns
Or rain to a land in drouth.

I would that your mother had never borne
Your father's seed to fruit,
That meadow rats had gnawed his corn
Before it gathered root.

Countee Cullen (1903–46)

Any Human to Another

The ills I sorrow at
Not me alone
Like an arrow,
Pierce to the marrow,
Through the fat
And past the bone.

Your grief and mine
Must intertwine
Like sea and river,
Be fused and mingle,
Diverse yet single,
Forever and forever.

Let no man be so proud
And confident,
To think he is allowed
A little tent
Pitched in a meadow
Of sun and shadow
All his little own.

Joy may be shy, unique,
Friendly to a few,
Sorrow may be scorned to speak
To any who
Were false or true.
Your every grief
Like a blade
Shining and unsheathed

Must strike me down.
Of bitter aloes wreathed,
My sorrow must be laid
On your head like a crown

Countee Cullen (1903–46)

Frigid and sweet Her parting Face –

Frigid and sweet Her parting Face –
Frigid and fleet my Feet –
Alien and vain whatever Clime
Acrid whatever Fate.

Given to me without the Suit
Riches and Name and Realm –
Who was She to withhold from me
Penury and Home?

Emily Dickinson (1830–86)

Now I knew I lost her –

Now I knew I lost her –
Not that she was gone –
But Remoteness travelled
On her Face and Tongue.

Alien, though adjoining
As a Foreign Race –
Traversed she though pausing
Latitudeless Place.

Elements Unaltered –
Universe the same
But Love's transmigration –
Somehow this had come –

Henceforth to remember
Nature took the Day
I had paid so much for –
His is Penury

Not who toils for Freedom
Or for Family
But the Restitution
Of Idolatry.

Emily Dickinson (1830–86)

Prove It On Me

Went out last night, had a great big fight
Everything seemed to go on wrong
I looked up, to my surprise
The gal I was with was gone

Where she went, I don't know
I mean to follow everywhere she goes;
Folks say I'm crooked. I didn't know where she took it
I want the whole world to know

They say I do it, ain't nobody caught me
Sure got to prove it on me;
Went out last night with a crowd of my friends
They must've been women, 'cause I don't like no men

It's true I wear a collar and a tie
Makes the wind blow all the while
Don't you say I do it, ain't nobody caught me
You sure got to prove it on me

Say I do it, ain't nobody caught me
Sure got to prove it on me
I went out last night with a crowd of my friends
It must've been women, 'cause I don't like no men

Wear my clothes just like a fan
Talk to the gals just like any old man
Cause they say I do it, ain't nobody caught me
Sure got to prove it on me

Ma Rainey (1886–1939)

The Ballad of Reading Gaol (extract)

In Debtors' Yard the stones are hard,
And the dripping wall is high,
So it was there he took the air
Beneath the leaden sky,
And by each side a Warder walked,
For fear the man might die.

Or else he sat with those who watched
His anguish night and day;
Who watched him when he rose to weep,
And when he crouched to pray;
Who watched him lest himself should rob
Their scaffold of its prey.

The Governor was strong upon
The Regulations Act:
The Doctor said that Death was but
A scientific fact:
And twice a day the Chaplain called,
And left a little tract.

And twice a day he smoked his pipe,
And drank his quart of beer:

His soul was resolute, and held
No hiding-place for fear;
He often said that he was glad
The hangman's hands were near.
But why he said so strange a thing
No Warder dared to ask:
For he to whom a watcher's doom
Is given as his task,
Must set a lock upon his lips,
And make his face a mask.
Or else he might be moved, and try
To comfort or console:
And what should Human Pity do
Pent up in Murderers' Hole?
What word of grace in such a place
Could help a brother's soul?

Oscar Wilde (1854–1900)

Out at Sea

The sea was witness of the words you said:
She hushed her every tide that she might hear
Your whispered love, and while you bent so near
My bosom, laying down your weary head
To rest thereon–the corals in their bed
Stirred with emotion, shaken as with fear,
And foam grew paler, passionately drear
As some wan smile, upon a face that's dead.
I took your hand in mine, your living hand!
And pressed it closer, closer in mine own.
A nameless terror shocked me while I scanned
Your ardent face; there rose a stifled moan
To part my lips; I saw the future stand
Before me, and behold! I was alone.

Radclyffe Hall (1880–1943)

Speculation

If at some future day we two should meet,
Stand face to face before the staring crowd,
And pull from Love's dead form the decent shroud
That time has wound about from head to feet—
I scarcely know what words would come to greet
Your presence, if they would be soft or loud,
Would your head be held high or humbly bowed,
And would the moment bitter be or sweet
To me, as you pushed back the long past years,
Would I rejoice, perhaps, at this new pain?
At least 'twould mean that I could live again,
And had not washed away my soul with tears.
I think there might be much that I could bless
In that deliverance out of nothingness.

Radclyffe Hall (1880–1943)

The Scar

Upon my life I bear one precious scar:
Each night I kiss it, till anew it bleeds,
And tell each drop of blood, as hallowed beads
Are told by those dear few who faithful are.
To me it seems to beautify, not mar,
My inner self, for from that deep wound leads
A path to gained respect, my secret needs
Quenched by the bleeding of that fountain are.
The fiery contest when that wound was won,
Still burns within my brain, and robs of life,
And terror, every lesser hurt that's done
To heart or spirit; let all harm run rife.
I shall not fear again to look upon
The gleaming edges of Fate's sharpest knife.

Radclyffe Hall (1880–1943)

We Two

What have we missed, we two–
You and I–I and you–
Of sorrow, and pain, and tears,
Of doubt, and of passionate fears,
Of madness, and badness, these years!
And what have we missed, we two!
But what have we missed, we two–
You and I–I and you–
Of rapture, and vast delight,
Of loving, and living, of right
To surrender, that love may requite,
How much have we missed, we two!

Radclyffe Hall (1880–1943)

The Affectionate Shepherd (extract)

The Teares of an Affectionate Shepheard Sick for Love,
Or the Complain of Daphnis for the Love of Ganimede

Scarce had the morning starre hid from the light
Heavens crimson canopie with stars bespangled,
But I began to rue th' unhappy sight
Of that faire boy that had my hart intangled;
Cursing the time, the place, the sense, the sin;
I came, I saw, I viewd, I slipped in.

If it be sinne to love a sweet-fac'd boy,
Whose amber locks trust up in golden tramels
Dangle adowne his lovely cheekes with joy,
When pearle and flowers his faire haire enamels;
If it be sinne to love a lovely lad,
Oh then sinne I, for whom my soule is sad.

His ivory-white and alabaster skin
Is staind throughout with rare vermillion red,
Whose twinckling starrie lights doe never blin
To shine on lovely Venus, Beauties bed;

But as the lillie and the blushing rose,
So white and red on him in order growes.

Upon a time the nymphs bestird them-selves
To trie who could his beautie soonest win;
But he accounted them but all as elves,
Except it were the faire Queene Guendolen:
Her he embrac'd, of her was beloved,
With plaints he proved, and with teares he moved.

But her an old man had beene sutor too,
That in his age began to doate againe;
Her would he often pray, and often woo,
When through old age enfeebled was his braine:
But she before had lov'd a lustie youth,
That now was dead, the cause of all her ruth.

And thus it hapned, Death and Cupid met
Upon a time at swilling Bacchus house,
Where daintie cates upon the boord were set,
And goblets full of wine to drinke carouse:
Where Love and Death did love the licor so,
That out they fall and to the fray they goe.

And having both their quivers at their backe
Fild full of arrows; th' one of fatall steele,
The other all of gold; Deaths shaft was black,
But Loves was yellow: Fortune turnd her wheele,
And from Deaths quiver fell a fatall shaft,
That under Cupid by the winde was waft.

And at the same time by ill hap there fell
Another arrow out of Cupids quiver,
The which was carried by the winde at will,
And under Death the amorous shaft did shiver:
They being parted, Love tooke up Deaths dart,
And Death tooke up Loves arrow for his part.

Thus as they wandred both about the world,
At last Death met with one of feeble age:
Wherewith he drew a shaft and at him hurld
The unknowne arrow with a furious rage,
Thinking to strike him dead with Deaths blacke dart;
But he, alas, with Love did wound his hart!

Richard Barnfield (1574–1627)

Sonnet 16

Long have I long'd to see my love againe,
Still have I wisht, but never could obtaine it;
Rather than all the world (if I might gaine it)
Would I desire my love's sweet precious gaine.
Yet in my soule I see him everie day,
See him, and see his still sterne countenaunce,
But (ah) what is of long continuance,
Where majestie and beautie beares the sway?
Sometimes, when I imagine that I see him,
(As love is full of foolish fantasies)
Weening to kisse his lips, as my love's fees,
I feele but aire: nothing but aire to bee him.
Thus with Ixion, kisse I clouds in vaine:
Thus with Ixion, feele I endles paine.

Richard Barnfield (1574–1627)

Alexis (extract from Eclogue II)

The shepherd Corydon with love was fired
For fair Alexis, his own master's joy:
No room for hope had he, yet, none the less,
The thick-leaved shadowy-soaring beech-tree grove
Still would he haunt, and there alone, as thus,
To woods and hills pour forth his artless strains.
'Cruel Alexis, heed you naught my songs?
Have you no pity? you'll drive me to my death.
Now even the cattle court the cooling shade
And the green lizard hides him in the thorn:
Now for tired mowers, with the fierce heat spent,
Pounds Thestilis her mess of savoury herbs,
Wild thyme and garlic. I, with none beside,
Save hoarse cicalas shrilling through the brake,
Still track your footprints 'neath the broiling sun.
Better have borne the petulant proud disdain
Of Amaryllis, or Menalcas wooed,
Albeit he was so dark, and you so fair!
Trust not too much to colour, beauteous boy;
White privets fall, dark hyacinths are culled.
You scorn me, Alexis, who or what I am

Care not to ask- how rich in flocks, or how
In snow-white milk abounding: yet for me
Roam on Sicilian hills a thousand lambs;
Summer or winter, still my milk-pails brim.
I sing as erst Amphion of Circe sang,
What time he went to call his cattle home
On Attic Aracynthus. Nor am I
So ill to look on: lately on the beach
I saw myself, when winds had stilled the sea,
And, if that mirror lie not, would not fear
Daphnis to challenge, though yourself were judge.
Ah! were you but content with me to dwell.
Some lowly cot in the rough fields our home,
Shoot down the stags, or with green osier-wand
Round up the straggling flock! There you with me
In silvan strains will learn to rival Pan.

Virgil (70–19 BC)

Shadwell Stair

I am the ghost of Shadwell Stair.
Along the wharves by the water-house,
And through the cavernous slaughter-house,
I am the shadow that walks there.

Yet I have flesh both firm and cool,
And eyes tumultuous as the gems
Of moons and lamps in the full Thames
When dusk sails wavering down the pool.

Shuddering the purple street-arc burns
Where I watch always; from the banks
Dolorously the shipping clanks
And after me a strange tide turns.

I walk till the stars of London wane
And dawn creeps up the Shadwell Stair.
But when the crowing syrens blare
I with another ghost am lain.

Wilfred Owen (1893–1918)

GREATER LOVE

Red lips are not so red
As the stained stones kissed by the English dead.
Kindness of wooed and wooer
Seems shame to their love pure.
O Love, your eyes lose lure
When I behold eyes blinded in my stead!

Your slender attitude
Trembles not exquisite like limbs knife-skewed,
Rolling and rolling there
Where God seems not to care;
Till the fierce love they bear
Cramps them in death's extreme decrepitude.

Your voice sings not so soft,–
Though even as wind murmuring through raftered loft,–
Your dear voice is not dear,
Gentle, and evening clear,
As theirs whom none now hear,
Now earth has stopped their piteous mouths that coughed.

Heart, you were never hot
Nor large, nor full like hearts made great with shot;
And though your hand be pale,
Paler are all which trail
Your cross through flame and hail:
Weep, you may weep, for you may touch them not.

Wilfred Owen (1893–1918)

PAUL'S CASE (EXTRACT)

It was Paul's afternoon to appear before the faculty of the Pittsburg High School to account for his various misdemeanors. He had been suspended a week ago, and his father had called at the principal's office and confessed his perplexity about his son. Paul entered the faculty room, suave and smiling. His clothes were a trifle outgrown, and the tan velvet on the collar of his open overcoat was frayed and worn; but, for all that, there was something of the dandy about him, and he wore an opal pin in his neatly knotted black four-in-hand, and a red carnation in his buttonhole. This latter adornment the faculty somehow felt was not properly significant of the contrite spirit befitting a boy under the ban of suspension. Paul was tall for his age and very thin, with high, cramped shoulders and a narrow chest. His eyes were remarkable for a certain hysterical brilliancy, and he continually used them in a conscious, theatrical sort of way, peculiarly offensive in a boy. The pupils were abnormally large, as though he were addicted to belladonna, but there was a glassy glitter about them which that drug does not produce.

When questioned by the principal as to why he was

there, Paul stated, politely enough, that he wanted to come back to school. This was a lie, but Paul was quite accustomed to lying–found it, indeed, indispensible for overcoming friction. His teachers were asked to state their respective charges, which they did with such a rancour and aggrievedness as evinced that this was not a usual case. Disorder and impertinence were among the offences named, yet each of his instructors felt that it was scarcely possible to put into words the real cause of the trouble, which lay in a sort of hysterically defiant manner of the boy's; in the contempt which they all knew he felt for them, and which he seemingly made not the least effort to conceal.

Willa Cather (1873–1947)

L'Envoi

Where are the loves that we have loved before
When once we are alone, and shut the door?
No matter whose the arms that held me fast,
The arms of Darkness hold me at the last.
No matter down what primrose path I tend,
I kiss the lips of Silence in the end.
No matter on what heart I found delight,
I come again unto the breast of Night.
No matter when or how love did befall,
'Tis Loneliness that loves me best of all,
And in the end she claims me, and I know
That she will stay, though all the rest may go.
No matter whose the eyes that I would keep
Near in the dark, 'tis in the eyes of Sleep
That I must look and look forever more,
When once I am alone, and shut the door.

Willa Cather (1873–1947)

Aftermath

Can'st thou conjure a vanished morn of spring,
Or bid the ashes of the sunset glow
Again to redness? Are we strong to wring
From trodden grapes the juice drunk long ago?
Can leafy longings stir in Autumn's blood,
Or can I wear a pearl dissolved in wine,
Or go a-Maying in a winter wood,
Or paint with youth thy wasted cheek, or mine?
What bloom, then, shall abide, since ours hath sped?
Thou art more lost to me than they who dwell
In Egypt's sepulchres, long ages fled;
And would I touch–Ah me! I might as well
Covet the gold of Helen's vanished head,
Or kiss back Cleopatra from the dead!

Willa Cather (1873–1947)

Identity & Acceptance

Sappho (extract from On the Cliffs)

Love's priestess, mad with pain and joy of song,
Song's priestess, mad with joy and pain of love,
Name above all names that are lights above,
We have lov'd, prais'd, pitied, crown'd, and done thee wrong,
O thou past praise and pity; thou the sole
Utterly deathless, perfect only and whole
Immortal, body and soul.
For over all whom time hath overpast
The shadow of sleep inexorable is cast,
The implacable sweet shadow of perfect sleep
That gives not back what life gives death to keep;
Yea, all that liv'd and lov'd and sang and sinn'd
Are all borne down death's cold, sweet, soundless wind
That blows all night and knows not whom its breath,
Darkling, may touch to death:
But one that wind hath touch'd and changed not,—one
Whose body and soul are parcel of the sun;
One that earth's fire could burn not, nor the sea
Quench; nor might human doom take hold on thee;
All praise, all pity, all dreams have done thee wrong,
All love, with eyes love-blinded from above;

Song's priestess, mad with joy and pain of love,
Love's priestess, mad with pain and joy of song.

Hast thou none other answer then for me
Than the air may have of thee,
Or the earth's warm woodlands girdling with green girth
Thy secret, sleepless, burning life on earth,
Or even the sea that once, being woman crown'd
And girt with fire and glory of anguish round,
Thou wert so fain to seek to, fain to crave
If she would hear thee and save
And give thee comfort of thy great green grave?
Because I have known thee always who thou art,
Thou knowest, have known thee to thy heart's own heart,
Nor ever have given light ear to storied song
That did thy sweet name sweet unwitting wrong,
Nor ever have call'd thee nor would call for shame,
Thou knowest, but inly by thine only name,
Sappho – because I have known thee and lov'd, hast thou
None other answer now?
As brother and sister were we, child and bird,
Since thy first Lesbian word
Flam'd on me, and I knew not whence I knew,

This was the song that struck my whole soul through,
Pierced my keen spirit of sense with edge more keen,
Even when I knew not, – even ere sooth was seen, –
When thou wast but the tawny sweet wing'd thing
Whose cry was but of spring.

Algernon Charles Swinburne (1837–1909)

Joseph and His Friend: A Story of Pennsylvania (extract)

'Is there no way out of this labyrinth of wrong?' Philip exclaimed. 'Two natures, as far apart as Truth and Falsehood, monstrously held together in the most intimate, the holiest of bonds,–two natures destined for each other monstrously kept apart by the same bonds! Is life to be so sacrificed to habit and prejudice? I said that Faith, like Law, was fashioned for the average man: then there must be a loftier faith, a juster law, for the men – and the women – who cannot shape themselves according to the commonplace pattern of society, – who were born with instincts, needs, knowledge, and rights – ay, rights! – of their own!'

Bayard Taylor (1825–78)

I Know My Soul

I plucked my soul out of its secret place,
And held it to the mirror of my eye,
To see it like a star against the sky,
A twitching body quivering in space,
A spark of passion shining on my face.
And I explored it to determine why
This awful key to my infinity
Conspires to rob me of sweet joy and grace.
And if the sign may not be fully read,
If I can comprehend but not control,
I need not gloom my days with futile dread,
Because I see a part and not the whole.
Contemplating the strange, I'm comforted
By this narcotic thought: I know my soul.

Claude McKay (1889–1948)

BAPTISM

Into the furnace let me go alone;
Stay you without in terror of the heat.
I will go naked in – for thus 'tis sweet –
Into the weird depths of the hottest zone.
I will not quiver in the frailest bone,
You will not note a flicker of defeat;
My heart shall tremble not its fate to meet,
My mouth give utterance to any moan.
The yawning oven spits forth fiery spears;
Red aspish tongues shout wordlessly my name.
Desire destroys, consumes my mortal fears,
Transforming me into a shape of flame.
I will come out, back to your world of tears,
A stronger soul within a finer frame.

Claude McKay (1889–1948)

I Have a Rendezvous with Life

I have a rendezvous with Life,
In days I hope will come,
Ere youth has sped, and strength of mind,
Ere voices sweet grow dumb.
I have a rendezvous with Life,
When Spring's first heralds hum.
Sure some would cry it's better far
To crown their days with sleep
Than face the road, the wind and rain,
To heed the calling deep.
Though wet nor blow nor space I fear,
Yet fear I deeply, too,
Lest Death should meet and claim me ere
I keep Life's rendezvous.

Countee Cullen (1903–46)

An Epitaph

(for Amy Lowell)

She leans across a golden table,
Confronts God with an eye
Still puzzled by the standard label
All flesh bears: Made to die–
And questions Him if He is able
To reassure her why.

Countee Cullen (1903-46)

Fruit of the Flower

My father is a quiet man
With sober, steady ways;
For simile, a folded fan;
His nights are like his days.
My mother's life is puritan,
No hint of cavalier,
A pool so calm you're sure it can
Have little depth to fear.

And yet my father's eyes can boast
How full his life has been;
There haunts them yet the languid ghost
Of some still sacred sin.

And though my mother chants of God,
And of the mystic river,
I've seen a bit of checkered sod
Set all her flesh aquiver.

Why should he deem it pure mischance
A son of his is fain

To do a naked tribal dance
Each time he hears the rain?

Why should she think it devil's art
That all my songs should be
Of love and lovers, broken heart,
And wild sweet agony?

Who plants a seed begets a bud,
Extract of that same root;
Why marvel at the hectic blood
That flushes this wild fruit?

Countee Cullen (1903–46)

The Intermediate Sex (extract)

Eros is a great leveler. Perhaps the true Democracy rests, more firmly than anywhere else, on a sentiment which easily passes the bounds of class and caste, and unites in the closest affection the most estranged ranks of society.

Edward Carpenter (1844–1929)

The Intermediate Sex (extract)

In its various forms, so far as we know them, Love seems always to have a deep significance and a most practical importance to us little mortals. In one form, as the mere semi-conscious Sex-love, which runs through creation and is common to the lowest animals and plants, it appears as a kind of organic basis for the unity of all creatures; in another, as the love of the mother for her offspring–which may also be termed a passion–it seems to pledge itself to the care and guardianship of the future race; in another, as the marriage of man and woman, it becomes the very foundation of human society. And so we can hardly believe that in its homogenic form, with which we are here concerned, it has not also a deep significance, and social uses and functions which will become clearer to us, the more we study it.

To some perhaps it may appear a little strained to place this last-mentioned form of attachment on a level of importance with the others, and such persons may be inclined to deny to the homogenic or homosexual love that intense, that penetrating, and at times overmastering character which would entitle it to rank as a great human passion. But in truth this view, when entertained, arises from a want of acquaintance with the actual facts; and it may not be amiss here, in the briefest possible way, to indicate what the world's History, Literature, and Art has to say to us on this aspect of the subject, before going on to further considerations. Certainly, if the confronting of danger and the endurance of pain and distress for the sake of the loved one, if sacrifice, unswerving devotion and life-long union, constitute proofs of the reality and intensity (and let us say healthiness) of an affection, then these proofs have been given in numberless cases of such attachment, not only as existing between men, but as between women, since the world began. The records of chivalric love, the feats of enamoured knights for their ladies' sakes, the stories of Hero and Leander, etc., are easily paralleled, if not surpassed, by the stories of the Greek comrades-in-arms and tyrannicides…The annals of all nations contain similar records–though probably among none has the ideal of this love been quite so enthusiastic and heroic as among the post-Homeric Greeks.

Edward Carpenter (1844–1929)

I dwell in Possibility –

I dwell in Possibility –
A fairer House than Prose –
More numerous of Windows –
Superior – for Doors –

Of Chambers as the Cedars –
Impregnable of eye –
And for an everlasting Roof
The Gambrels of the Sky –

Of Visitors – the fairest –
For Occupation – This –
The spreading wide my narrow Hands
To gather Paradise –

Emily Dickinson (1830–86)

I am afraid to own a Body

I am afraid to own a Body –
I am afraid to own a Soul –
Profound – precarious Property –
Possession, not optional –

Double Estate – entailed at pleasure
Upon an unsuspecting Heir –
Duke in a moment of Deathlessness
And God, for a Frontier.

Emily Dickinson (1830–86)

JAMES BALDWIN ON SEXUALITY

Everybody's journey is individual. You don't know with whom you're going to fall in love. … If you fall in love with a boy, you fall in love with a boy. The fact that many Americans consider it a disease says more about them than it does about homosexuality.

James Baldwin (1947–85)

Autobiography of an Androgyne (extract)

The How of a double life during this period of my career will now be described. On the eve of one of my fortnightly female-impersonation sprees, the reader probably supposes that I would be happy in anticipation. On the contrary, a great weight of sorrow and anxiety always oppressed me. There was of course an attraction which drew me to the city, but it was more than counterbalanced by the realization of the risks of my losing my then enviable position in life, and the dread of the danger I had to put myself in, in order to obtain the satisfaction of my instincts. A peculiar phenomenon was vivid images of violent blows in the face, since I had been the victim of such a number of times. But even apart from the dread of the real dangers, even if there were no such dangers, an overwhelming feeling of sadness and anxiety always came over me as the time to go forth on my peculiar quest approached. On the eve of a female-impersonation spree during this period, I always felt like a soldier on entering a great battle from which he realized he might never come back alive, or like a murderer on the eve of his electrocution. On such occasions I habitually sang to myself:

' Why oh why should we be melancholy, boys,
Whose business 'tis to die ? '

Just before leaving my residence, I always knelt and prayed the Heavenly Father to bring me back safe, and on my return likewise my first act was to thank Him for it. Arrived in New York, my melancholy and dread would almost entirely disappear, and in their place a sense of gladness would spring up that in the great metropolis I was lost to all who knew me. I was in the habit of putting up at a third-class hotel in a poor quarter of the city, registering under an assumed name. About eight in the evening, I would retire to my room, remove my outer clothing, conceal my valuables, dress myself in a rather shabby suit, and saunter forth, hurrying past hotel employees so that they would not observe my change of apparel. Reaching the Bowery or some other street among those named in the account of my 'low-class fairie ' period, I would experience a feeling of exultation at finding myself again on Jennie June's stamping ground.

Jennie June (1874–1921)

Autobiography of an Androgyne (extract)

'Judging from the past, my life is likely to be a wreck if I deny this instinctive craving. In leading a life of chastity, I have endured a melancholy existence, and have often deliberated suicide. Recently I have meditated it daily. All my privileges, which one would think must make my life a happy one, have failed to make life to me worth living. You may say it is my own fault, and that I just make my own life miserable. But truly, it is a matter to me not dependent on my will power, but on physiological and psychological laws, over which the will has no more control than over the diphtheria.

'That I desire such indulgence does not spring from the fact that I have become licentious or a debauchee, placing my own selfish sensual enjoyment above everything else. I am as ardent as ever in my yearnings to alleviate human misery and to deny myself for others. But in this matter, the result of my denying myself would be almost as serious as to resolve to give up eating for the sake of saving the money for the cause of missions. There are some things which it would be fatal to us to give up, even if we did it through motives of altruism. I assure you that I have not abandoned my high aspirations and worthy aims of life.

'I assert before God that I am confident that I commit no sin in obeying this instinct. During my moments of closest communion with God, I am sensible of His smile on my conduct in this matter. In general the only legitimate relations are between a legally married pair. The marriage state is open to the normal man and he is duty bound to marry when passion becomes too strong. This duty however is not binding on urnings, because they cannot get any one to marry them. I endeavored to marry a young man in New York, but failed. Therefore it is in consonance with the moral law for urnings to enjoy the company of those they love without marrying.

'You may reply that such relations are prohibited in the Bible. Relations between man and man, both of whom are normal, are prohibited. But in the past year I have learned that I am seven-eighths a woman, and only one-eighth man. Were it not for certain masculine conformations of the body, I ought to go about in dresses as a woman, and always identify myself with the female sex. Therefore, I being more a woman than a man, these prohibitions in the Bible do not apply to me.

'I think I have satisfied you that I can without sin follow out my desire in the way Nature prompts. But I would convince you that my companion also acquiesces in my desire without sin. I would not wish to allure any one into obliging me unless he could see that he was thereby committing no sin. There is sin only in those things which rob God of His glory, or which bring unhappiness and detriment to some sentient being. In this case, if sin at all, it would be sin against self. But by it you harm yourself in no way, as the physician told me.

'Then too, urnings, congenital as I, are the work of God, the divine purpose in their creation being probably to check a too rapid increase in the population; and God must therefore have meant that their instinctive cravings for a sexual counterpart should be gratified, especially since he has made these cravings doubly intense. But how could they be gratified without the acquiescence of some normal individual? Therefore the latter is also without sin.

'I am not now, as you may think, writing in a state of extreme excitement, such as I might be in in the presence of the attractive person, when I would not be my true self; but I am writing in a comparatively calm, rational frame of mind. I am backed up in what I write by an experienced physician, whose letter I can show you, and who says that if I had the occasional satisfaction of this craving, I would become healthy, get rid of my morbid thoughts, and have some vim for work, and for distinguishing myself as a scholar. I am myself confident that with this occasional gratification I would some day win the admiration of the circles of religion and learning for my scholarly attainments and for my work for humanity.

'All I ask is that you take a common-sense, rational view of the matter. If there is still any doubt in your mind about your possible compliance being compatible with honor and morality, please state your difficulty, and I assure you I can remove it, since I have given much study to the ethics of this question. . .'

Jennie June (1874–1921)

An Ideal Husband (extract)

To love oneself is the beginning of a lifelong romance.

Oscar Wilde (1854–1900)

A Welcome

Dear Ghost, across a wind-swept sphere
You wander back again to me,
And I am not afraid, for see
I bid you rest beside me here!
I press your icy lips to mine,
Since you and I are almost one
Can I condemn what you have done
To render fruitless the divine?
Some day perchance our weary task
May finish, and we two will stand
Before the Maker, hand in hand,
There will be much that we shall ask!

Radclyffe Hall (1880–1943)

Incompatible

To-day I hate that bitter creed,
Whereby the groaning soul is taught
That God Almighty finds the need
Of pain, ere true salvation's wrought!

Dear God, who did create the trees,
The scented flowers, the misty view,
The uplands' breezy ecstasies,
The Ocean's iridescent blue,

The arches of the endless sky,
The magic of a day in Spring,
The down upon a butterfly,
The anthem that the skylarks sing.

All perfect growing harmonies,
Each tuneful sound and beauteous sight,
That lifts us from our miseries
To raptures of supreme delight,

Can I believe that Thou hast willed
Each bitter moment I have spent?

Whereby in anguish were fulfilled
Thy hard decrees of punishment?

To-day is June! Since early dawn
My heart has felt the sun's caress,
I bless the hour that I was born
To witness so much loveliness.

And I would have a God of love,
A tender God, who looks and smiles
From some not distant throne above
Upon His fair created miles.

I know not who has placed the thorns
That pierce, on our human brow,
But I would pray on these sweet morns.
Dear God, Oh! Let it not be Thou.

Radclyffe Hall (1880–1943)

My Choice

I have chosen a hill very solemn and tall,
To shelter me.
I have chosen a home very humble and small,
Where I would be.

I have chosen a wind very fragrant and gay,
To kiss my mouth.
I have chosen a view, stretching ever away,
When I look south.

I have chosen a glow that the sunlight shall bring
When morning calls.
I have chosen a choir of the thrushes to sing
When twilight falls.

I have chosen a shrine where my spirit may pray,
Blessing its birth.
I have chosen a breast where my head I can lay,
Sweet Mother Earth!

Radclyffe Hall (1880–1943)

Orlando (extract)

He stretched himself. He rose. He stood upright in complete nakedness before us, and while the trumpets pealed Truth! Truth! Truth! we have no choice left but confess — he was a woman.

The sound of the trumpets died away and Orlando stood stark naked. No human being, since the world began, has ever looked more ravishing. His form combined in one the strength of a man and a woman's grace. As he stood there, the silver trumpets prolonged their note, as if reluctant to leave the lovely sight which their blast had called forth; and Chastity, Purity, and Modesty, inspired, no doubt, by Curiosity, peeped in at the door and threw a garment like a towel at the naked form which, unfortunately, fell short by several inches. Orlando looked himself up and down in a long looking-glass, without showing any signs of discomposure, and went, presumably, to his bath.

We may take advantage of this pause in the narrative to make certain statements. Orlando had become a woman – there is no denying it. But in every other respect, Orlando remained precisely as he had been. The change of sex, though it altered their future, did nothing whatever to alter their identity. Their faces remained, as their portraits prove, practically the same. His memory – but in future we must, for convention's sake, say 'her' for 'his,' and 'she' for 'he'– her memory then, went back through all the events of her past life without encountering any obstacle. Some slight haziness there may have been, as if a few dark drops had fallen into the clear pool of memory; certain things had become a little dimmed; but that was all. The change seemed to have been accomplished painlessly and completely and in such a way that Orlando herself showed no surprise at it. Many people, taking this into account, and holding that such a change of sex is against nature, have been at great pains to prove (1) that Orlando had always been a woman, (2) that Orlando is at this moment a man. Let biologists and psychologists determine. It is enough for us to state the simple fact; Orlando was a man till the age of thirty; when he became a woman and has remained so ever since. But let other pens treat of sex and sexuality; we quit such odious subjects as soon as we can. Orlando had now washed, and dressed herself in those Turkish coats and trousers which can be worn indifferently by either sex; and was forced to consider her position. That it was precarious and embarrassing in the extreme must be the first thought of every reader who has followed her story with sympathy. Young, noble, beautiful, she had woken to find herself in a position than which we can conceive none more delicate for a young lady of rank. We should not have blamed her had she rung the bell, screamed, or fainted. But Orlando showed no such signs of perturbation. All her actions were deliberate in the extreme, and might indeed have been thought to show tokens of premeditation. First, she carefully examined the papers on the table; took such as seemed to be written in poetry, and secreted them in her bosom; next she called her Seleuchi hound, which had never left her bed all these days, though half famished with hunger, fed and combed him; then stuck a pair of pistols in her belt; finally wound about her person several strings of emeralds and pearls of the finest orient which had formed part of her Ambassadorial wardrobe. This done, she leant out of the window, gave one low whistle, and descended the shattered and bloodstained staircase, now strewn with the litter of waste-paper baskets, treaties, despatches, seals, sealing wax, etc., and so entered the courtyard. There, in the shadow of a giant fig tree, waited an old gipsy on a donkey. He led another by the bridle. Orlando swung her leg over it; and thus, attended by a lean dog, riding a donkey, in company of a gipsy, the Ambassador of Great Britain at the Court of the Sultan left Constantinople.

They rode for several days and nights and met with a variety of adventures, some at the hands of men, some at the hands of nature, in all of which Orlando acquitted herself with courage. Within a week they reached the high ground outside Broussa, which was then the chief camping ground of the gipsy tribe to which Orlando had allied herself. Often she had looked at those mountains from her balcony at the Embassy; often had longed to be there; and to find oneself where one has longed to be always, to a reflective mind, gives food for thought. For some time, however, she was too well pleased with the change to spoil it by thinking. The pleasure of having no documents to seal or sign, no flourishes to make, no calls to pay, was enough.

Virginia Woolf (1882–1941)

Song of Myself: 3

I have heard what the talkers were talking, the talk of the
  beginning and the end
But I do not talk of the beginning or the end.

There was never any more inception than there is now,
Nor any more youth or age than there is now,
And will never be any more perfection than there is now,
Nor any more heaven or hell than there is now.

Urge and urge and urge,
Always the procreant urge of the world.

Out of the dimness opposite equals advance, always
substance and increase, always sex,
Always a knit of identity, always distinction, always a breed
  of life.
To elaborate is no avail, learn'd and unlearn'd feel that it is so.

Sure as the most certain sure, plumb in the uprights, well
  entretied, braced in the beams,

Stout as a horse, affectionate, haughty, electrical,
I and this mystery here we stand.

Clear and sweet is my soul, and clear and sweet is all that is not my soul.

Lack one lacks both, and the unseen is proved by the seen,
Till that becomes unseen and receives proof in its turn.

Showing the best and dividing it from the worst age vexes age,
Knowing the perfect fitness and equanimity of things, while they discuss I am silent, and go bathe and admire myself.

Welcome is every organ and attribute of me, and of any man hearty and clean,
Not an inch nor a particle of an inch is vile, and none shall be less familiar than the rest.

I am satisfied–I see, dance, laugh, sing;
As the hugging and loving bed-fellow sleeps at my side through the night, and withdraws at the peep of the day with stealthy tread.

Leaving me baskets cover'd with white towels swelling the
    house with their plenty,
Shall I postpone my acceptation and realization and scream
    at my eyes,
That they turn from gazing after and down the road,
And forthwith cipher and show me to a cent,
Exactly the value of one and exactly the value of two, and
which is ahead?

Walt Whitman (1819–92)

Song of Myself: 24

Walt Whitman, a kosmos, of Manhattan the son,
Turbulent, fleshy, sensual, eating, drinking and breeding,
No sentimentalist, no stander above men and women or
    apart from them,
No more modest than immodest.

Unscrew the locks from the doors!
Unscrew the doors themselves from their jambs!

Whoever degrades another degrades me,
And whatever is done or said returns at last to me.

Through me the afflatus surging and surging, through me
    the current and index.

I speak the pass-word primeval, I give the sign of democracy,
By God! I will accept nothing which all cannot have their
    counterpart of on the same terms.

Through me many long dumb voices,
Voices of the interminable generations of prisoners and slaves,

Voices of the diseas'd and despairing and of thieves and dwarfs,
Voices of cycles of preparation and accretion,
And of the threads that connect the stars, and of wombs
    and of the father-stuff,
And of the rights of them the others are down upon,
Of the deform'd, trivial, flat, foolish, despised,
Fog in the air, beetles rolling balls of dung.

Through me forbidden voices,
Voices of sexes and lusts, voices veil'd and I remove the veil,
Voices indecent by me clarified and transfigur'd.

I do not press my fingers across my mouth,
I keep as delicate around the bowels as around the head
    and heart,
Copulation is no more rank to me than death is.

I believe in the flesh and the appetites,
Seeing, hearing, feeling, are miracles, and each part and
    tag of me is a miracle.

Divine am I inside and out, and I make holy whatever I
 touch or am touch'd from,
The scent of these arm-pits aroma finer than prayer,
This head more than churches, bibles, and all the creeds.
If I worship one thing more than another it shall be the
 spread of my own body, or any part of it,
Translucent mould of me it shall be you!
Shaded ledges and rests it shall be you!
Firm masculine colter it shall be you!
Whatever goes to the tilth of me it shall be you!
You my rich blood! your milky stream pale strippings of
 my life!
Breast that presses against other breasts it shall be you!
My brain it shall be your occult convolutions!
Root of wash'd sweet-flag! timorous pond-snipe! nest of
 guarded duplicate eggs! it shall be you!
Mix'd tussled hay of head, beard, brawn, it shall be you!
Trickling sap of maple, fibre of manly wheat, it shall
 be you!
Sun so generous it shall be you!

Vapors lighting and shading my face it shall be you!
You sweaty brooks and dews it shall be you!
Winds whose soft-tickling genitals rub against me it shall
 be you!
Broad muscular fields, branches of live oak, loving lounger
in my winding paths, it shall be you!
Hands I have taken, face I have kiss'd, mortal I have ever
 touch'd, it shall be you.

I dote on myself, there is that lot of me and all so luscious,
Each moment and whatever happens thrills me with joy,
I cannot tell how my ankles bend, nor whence the cause of
my faintest wish,
Nor the cause of the friendship I emit, nor the cause of the
 friendship I take again.

That I walk up my stoop, I pause to consider if it really be,
A morning-glory at my window satisfies me more than the
 metaphysics of books.

To behold the day-break!
The little light fades the immense and diaphanous shadows,
The air tastes good to my palate.

Hefts of the moving world at innocent gambols silently
    rising freshly exuding,
Scooting obliquely high and low.

Something I cannot see puts upward libidinous prongs,
Seas of bright juice suffuse heaven.
The earth by the sky staid with, the daily close of their
    junction,
The heav'd challenge from the east that moment over
    my head,
The mocking taunt, See then whether you shall be master!

Walt Whitman (1819–92)

INDEX

B
Baldwin, James
  James Baldwin on Sexuality 134
Barnfield, Richard
  'Sonnet 16' 108
  'Sonnet 17' 31
  'The Affectionate Shepherd' (Extract) 105

C
Carpenter, Edward
  The Intermediate Sex (Extract) 129
  The Intermediate Sex (Extract) 130
Cather, Willa
  'Aftermath' 117
  'L'Envoi' 116
  'Paul's Case' (Extract) 114
  'Sonnet 41'
Cullen, Countee
  'A Song of Sour Grapes' 91
  'An Epitaph' 126
  'Any Human to Another' 92
  'Epitaphs' 18
  'Fruit of the Flower' 127
  'I Have a Rendezvous with Life' 125
  'Tableau (for Donald Duff)' 61

D
Dickinson, Emily
  'Frigid and sweet Her parting Face –' 94
  'Her breast is fit for pearls' 67
  'I am afraid to own a Body' 133
  'I dwell in Possibility –' 132
  Letter to Susan Huntington Gilbert 63
  'Now I knew I lost her –' 95
  'Tell Her – the page I never wrote! (Version II)' 65
  'To own a Susan of my own' 68
  'Wild Nights – Wild Nights!' 20
Dunbar-Nelson, Alice
  'I Sit and Sew' 14
  'You! Inez!' 13

F
Field, Michael
  'A Girl' 74
  'It Was Deep April' 75
  'Unbosoming' 76
Forster, E.M.
  'E.M. Forster on Maurice' 62

H
Hall, Radclyffe
  'A Welcome' 142
  'House Hunting' 78
  'Incompatible' 143
  'My Choice' 145
  'One Night' 29
  'Out at Sea' 101
  'The Meeting' 80
  The Well of Loneliness (Extract) 81
  'Speculation' 102
  'The Scar' 103
  'To Some One!' 30
  'We Two' 104
Hermann, Fürst von Pückler-Muskau
  An Account of The Ladies of Llangollen (Extract) 71
Homer
  The Iliad (Extract) 26
Housman, A.E.
  'A Shropshire Lad – XLIV' 87
  'A Shropshire Lad – XV' 84
  'A Shropshire Lad – XVIII' 45
  'A Shropshire Lad – XXXVIII' 85
  'He would not stay for me, and who can wonder' 83

J
Jewsbury, Geraldine
  Letter to Jane Carlyle (Extract) 69
June, Jennie

Autobiography of an Androgyne (Extract) 135
Autobiography of an Androgyne (Extract) 137

L

Levy, Amy
'At a Dinner Party' 16
'On the Threshold' 89
Lowell, Amy
'A Decade' 47
'Hora Stellatrix' 46

M

McKay, Claude
'Absence' 58
'Alfonso, Dressing to Wait at a Table' 17
'Baptism' 124
'Courage' 60
'I Know My Soul' 123
'The Barrier' 90
'Tormented' 59
Mew, Charlotte
'On the Road to the Sea' 54

O

Owen, Wilfred
'Greater Love' 112
'Shadwell Stair' 111

R

Rainey, Ma
'Prove It On Me' 97

S

Sappho
'Ode to Anactoria' 32
'The Daughter of Cyprus' 34
Seward, Anna
'Llangollen Vale' (Extract) 48
Shakespeare, William
'Sonnet 20' 42
'Sonnet 144' 43
Stein, Gertrude
'Lifting Belly' (Extract) 21
'Pink Melon Joy' (Extract) 23
'Susie Asado' 25
Swinburne, Algernon Charles
'Anactoria' (Extract) 11
'Sappho' (Extract from On the Cliffs) 119

T

Taylor, Bayard
Joseph and His Friend: A Story of Pennsylvania (Extract) 50
Joseph and His Friend: A Story of Pennsylvania (Extract) 122
'Love Returned' 51

V

Virgil
'Alexis' (Extract from Eclogue II) 109

W

Whitman, Walt
'I Sing the Body Electric!' (Extract) 38
'Song of Myself: 3' 150
'Song of Myself: 11' (Extract) 36
'Song of Myself: 24' 153
Wilde, Oscar
An Ideal Husband (Extract) 141
'On the Sale By Auction of Keats' Love Letters' 77
'The Ballad of Reading Gaol' (Extract) 99
The Picture of Dorian Gray (Extract) 27
Woolf, Virginia
Orlando (Extract) 146